STAG DOS
AND
SPEECHES

STAG DOS
AND
SPEECHES

SOUND ADVICE FOR
SENDING YOUR
GROOM OFF
IN STYLE

Dominic Bliss

DOG 'n' BONE

To Sally. I wasn't best man, I was groom.

This edition published in 2019 by Dog 'n' Bone Books
an imprint of Ryland Peters & Small Ltd
20–21 Jockey's Fields
London WC1R 4BW

www.rylandpeters.com

10 9 8 7 6 5 4 3 2 1

First published in 2013 by Dog 'n' Bone Books

A CIP catalog record for this book is available from
the British Library.

ISBN: 978 1 911026 84 6

Printed in China

Editors: Tim Leng and Pete Jorgensen
Designer: Jerry Goldie
Illustrator: Kuo Kang Chen

CONTENTS

INTRODUCTION

DON'T PANIC!

You're slightly panicky, aren't you? You've been appointed best man, the wedding's not far off and you've now got to pull your finger out: there's a stag party to organise and a witty speech to write. Well, you can stop panicking. Help is at hand. Read this book and I guarantee that not only will you celebrate the end of the groom's bachelor life in style, but you'll also deliver a truly scintillating speech at the wedding reception.

WEDDING TRADITIONS

Wedding traditions may vary quite a bit across the English-speaking world, but when it comes to the best man, his basic duties will generally be pretty similar across the board.

1. You celebrate the groom's final days as a single man.
2. You help with the wedding rehearsal and organise the ushers.
3. You write and deliver a great speech at the wedding reception.

In North America, they call it a bachelor party. In the UK it's a stag party. Aussies enjoy a bucks party and South Africans tend to have a bull party. But it doesn't really matter what you call it (in France, they use the macabre term 'burial of the life of a boy') because the goal is always the same: get all the groom's friends together and throw a wild party. Just how wild is up to you.

All across the world it's traditional for the best man to make a speech at the wedding reception. There are no hard-and-fast rules as to the format or style of this speech, however. It often depends on how formal the wedding is. A few simple words and a toast will be fine for a Vegas shotgun wedding. But if it's a more refined affair you really should pull out all the stops and prepare a full-on oration.

In ancient times, the best man was expected to help the groom fight off members of the bride's family who were unhappy at having their girl snatched away. Fortunately, this practice is less common today.

THE BEST MAN SUITABILITY QUIZ

Find out if you're really the best man for the job. Take our multiple-choice best man test.

1. Your idea of smart is:
a. A tie without food stains on it.
b. A jacket and trousers that, if they don't exactly match, are at least similar in colour.
c. James Bond in a tuxedo.

2. Are you punctual?
a. Zzzzzzzzzzzzzzz…
b. Yes, but only after midday.
c. The early bird catches the worm.

3. How safe is the ring with you?
a. What ring?
b. Safe with Gollum, my precious.
c. On a chain around my neck or taped to my nether regions.

4. Your body reacts to booze as follows:
a. Two beers and you've passed out on the floor.
b. Beer after wine, everything's fine. Wine after beer and it's goodnight, my dear.
c. You could drink Ozzy Osbourne under the table.

5. Your idea of a wild night out is:

a. Scrabble at the retirement home.

b. Cow tipping.

c. Downing bottles of absinthe and defenestrating hotel televisions.

6. The best place for a £50 note is:

a. In a savings account.

b. Waved in front of a barman's nose.

c. Between a sexy lady's navel and her knicker elastic.

7. Your idea of a practical joke is:

a. Shaved genitals and a rude tattoo.

b. Being handcuffed to a lamp post.

c. Obligatory cross-dressing and a wig.

8. The bride-to-be asks you what you got up to on the stag party. You tell her:

a. The gospel truth.

b. 'What goes on tour, stays on tour.'

c. A total pack of lies, all with a straight face.

Your score

Mainly As: Perhaps you should hand over your duties to someone else.

Mainly Bs: Getting there, but you need to let your hair down a bit.

Mainly Cs: Sounds like you're the best best man in the world.

PART 1

THE STAG PARTY

PLANNING THE PARTY

In the old days, the best man's job was far simpler than it is now. It normally involved dragging the groom and his best friends down the local bar for an evening of booze and rude jokes.

Nowadays, you're expected to be much more adventurous. No self-respecting husband-to-be is going to celebrate his final night of freedom at the local pub. No way. These days you have to think of something more along the lines of a weekend in Vegas or Lithuania.

We're all getting married much later in life, which means we have more cash to spend on the stag party. Also, travel is so much easier. Whether it's a transatlantic jaunt to Vegas or a budget flight to eastern European, the world, my friend, is your oyster. Play your cards right and there will be a very large pearl inside.

But with so many stag party destinations to choose from, how do you decide where to go? And, more importantly, who to invite along?

The guest list

It's not as straightforward as a simple list of the groom's best mates. There are numerous political and logistical complications to think of. Will the groom's 'colourful' friend from football, Tony 'The Shark', really get on with Square Simon from

accounts? Will the groom's university mates have anything vaguely in common with his loutish cousins from Essex?

Discuss very prudently with the groom which of his friends he ought to invite. If they're going to split up into separate cliques during the weekend, that defeats the whole object of throwing the party in the first place. Remember, a stag party is all about helping the groom and his friends to bond together.

It's no easy task. You may well have to include a rag-tag mix of people from school, university, and work, plus the groom's brothers and maybe his future brother-in-law or possibly even his father and father-to-be. If you've ever seen the film *The Hangover*, you'll know what a can of worms the bride's side of the family could be.

Then there's the obligatory party wild card. Every stag party has one – the rogue element or loose cannon who risks exploding at any minute. You've got to be ready for that.

There are financial considerations, too. Say the groom works in The City. There's no way old friends from his home town will have the same amount of cash to splash as his work colleagues. While they may be happy to fly first class to Monaco for the weekend, it's unlikely anyone else will be able to afford it. This could cause serious embarrassment within the group.

A family affair?

What are the rules when it comes to inviting members of the groom's family? Should you ask his father, his brother or even (remember the bearded Zach Galifianakis in *The Hangover*?) his brother-in-law-to-be to join in the celebrations?

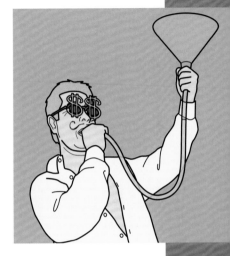

In the old days, it was quite common to bring the male contingent of the groom's family along on the stag do. Hang on a minute, though – do you really want the groom's father stuffing £10 notes into strippers' panties and shotgunning cans of beer? More to the point, do you want him watching you and the groom getting up to that kind of stuff?

No, of course you don't. Which is why old Pops should stay at home. And don't for a minute even think about inviting the groom's future father-in-law. Unless, of course, he's marrying Kelly Osbourne, in which case you can guarantee Ozzy will be the first name on the guest list and star of the party.

The trick is to warn everyone in advance exactly how much it's all going to cost. Then if it's way out of anyone's league, they can politely decline. You could even consider throwing two separate stag parties: a long weekend in Cancun for the groom's City trader friends, and a night at the local pub for everyone else. Perfectly acceptable.

PAYING FOR THE STAG PARTY

Stag parties need to be booked well in advance. You don't think the Golden Nugget in Las Vegas will reserve a suite without some sort of up-front deposit, do you? And there could be flights to pay for. Understandably, you won't be too keen to stump up for everything yourself.

Show me the money

Getting the cash together to pay for the stag party is where the headaches set in (and you haven't even done any drinking yet). To sort out all the finances, you're going to need the skills of a crime boss accountant. Start off by emailing everyone who's going on the stag party and warning them how much they will be expected to pay in total. Remember to include every possible expense in advance, since it's much easier to hit everyone with one large bill than lots of small ones. And don't forget to include the groom's expenses, too. Apart from flights – which the groom will often cover himself – he should be expecting to enjoy a free weekend courtesy of all his buddies.

Stag party expenses:

- Printed T-shirts and the groom's outfit
- Travel to and from the party destination
- Hotel rooms
- Daytime activities
- Restaurants
- Bar bills
- Nightclubs
- Taxis

Ask all the party members to transfer their individual cash contributions into your bank account. You want to make sure everyone has paid up before you book the various activities, otherwise you'll spend half the weekend hassling everyone to hand over the money and juggling bundles of cash. Not such a wise idea when you're stumbling about in a strange city with a few drinks inside you.

If the destination involves flights, then it all becomes a little bit more complicated. Ticket prices often rise sharply the closer you get to travel time. A budget flight from London to Prague can cost the same as a transatlantic long-haul if you leave it until the last minute. For this reason, it's often easier to tell everyone to pay for their own flights. Simply book yourself and the groom on a certain flight, and ensure all the other groomsmen follow suit.

Party organisers

They're expensive, but stag party organisers will save you a lot of time and effort. They will book everything in advance, and they always have great contacts within the leisure industry. There's also the added benefit that if anything goes wrong – say, you wake up with Mike Tyson's pet tiger in your hotel room, for example – you can always blame it on someone else.

Send out emails

It's good to warm up the groom and all his guests in the days leading up to the stag party, and the easiest way to do this is by sending a few emails to put people in the mood. Encourage them to get a bit of banter going, and to exaggerate about how they're planning numerous cruel practical jokes for the groom. While you don't want him to be so scared that he backs out at the last minute, there's nothing wrong with putting the wind up him slightly.

Of course, the stag party should contain an element of surprise for the groom, so with all the pre-party email banter, just make sure no one gives the game away. While he may have agreed on Cancun as the actual destination for the party, he shouldn't know that water-skiing and half-naked tequila cowgirls are on the cards. Surprises will make the weekend much more memorable.

Real-life groom

A few years back, an American groom decided to appoint his female cousin – whom he considered his best friend – as best man. Or best woman, rather. Of course, this raised a few eyebrows among his male friends. They were expecting dinosaur-hunting with machine guns... or something along those lines. But the groom knew she wouldn't let him down.

As a woman, she could hardly suggest tequila slammers at a strip club, but she did manage to come up with an ingenious solution. First off, she organised a football match involving all the men, with her good self as referee. Afterwards, to ease everyone's sore muscles, she booked a group session at a luxurious spa. This idea was initially dismissed by some of the groom's friends, who complained that it was a bit girly, but once they'd experienced a soothing massage, a steam bath and a jacuzzi, they soon changed their tune. For the evening's entertainment, the best woman had reserved a table at a top restaurant, and a rock gig at a local music venue. All the guys loved it.

Mixed-sex stag dos

Who says it has to be all boys? While it might not neccessarily be everyone's idea of the perfect send-off before married life, but in these days of political correctness you might well find yourself on a mixed stag/hen party. In fact, these combined events have become so common that a handy portmanteau has crept its way into modern parlance – the hag do. As best man, of course you'll have to make sure the groom doesn't misbehave in front of his wife-to-be. But let's face it, you're unlikely to have strippers (of either sex) at a mixed-sex party.

You may find yourself teaming up with the chief bridesmaid to organise the evening's proceedings. It sounds obvious, but bear in mind who you're catering for. Suddenly, a sports bar doesn't sound like such a great option. But then neither is an evening in the company of the Chippendales. What about a male-female-friendly compromise? How about miniature golf, go-karting and a slap-up meal in a restaurant? That's sure to keep everyone happy.

Keep the bride sweet

The bride-to-be is going to be very suspicious of you. After all, you're the man tasked with corrupting her future husband just days before she's due to marry him. Try your best to get into her good books.

There's no point lying through your teeth. She's not stupid. She knows alcohol and (possibly) exotic dancers will feature strongly during the stag party. But you need to smooth things over a bit. Reassure her that you're not planning some sort of Bacchanalian orgy, and that you'll bring her precious man home to her in one piece.

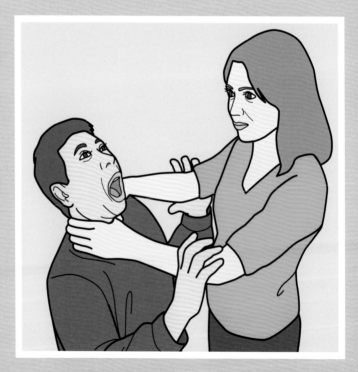

CHOOSING THE DESTINATION

In many years' time, when your groom is lying on his deathbed, he's certainly not going to thank you for staging his stag party in the Irish-themed pub at the bottom of his street. Come on – live a little! Why not head for the beach or the mountains? Or if all the ushers can afford the time and money, why not spend a weekend abroad? You don't have to fly halfway across the world, but there's nothing like a foreign culture and warmer climate to get the party going.

British stag party tradition has been totally transformed over the last decade or so thanks to the revolution in European short-haul airline travel. You can now get a flight from London to Lithuania or Estonia for the same price as the taxi ride to the airport. It's a similar situation in North America, with relatively cheap flights to Mexico and the Caribbean.

Outside of your home nation, you'll find everyone's inhibitions quickly evaporate, which can certainly help fuel the party spirit. And it

doesn't seem to hurt your wallet as much when you're flashing the cash in a foreign currency. Just make sure you stay on the right side of the local law. Your groom won't thank you if he's forced to spend the night in a Moscow jail, together with the local nutcase, having been charged with walking the streets in nothing but comedy fake breasts.

Air travel tips

Airport concourses aren't the most convivial of places. And, as best man, you hardly want to be running between terminals trying to rally everyone together. What about booking everyone into the first class lounge before the flight? That way you can really start the weekend in style with a few pre-flight drinks.

But be warned: flight crews are under strict instructions not to allow drunkards onto their flights, so keep the booze to a minimum before you fly, otherwise you won't be going anywhere.

Stag party bucket list

If money were absolutely no object, where would you go? Here are the world's flashiest party destinations.

Bangkok
Start off with cocktails at Sirocco, an open-air restaurant on the 64th floor of State Tower. The nighttime views from the Sky Bar are truly magnificent. Then head for Soi Cowboy or Patpong for a live show – and possibly some novel tips on serving a ping-pong ball.

Rio de Janeiro
Carnival time. Head for South America's most exciting city in February to guarantee the party of a lifetime. Then sleep off your hangover on Copacabana beach before taking on the locals in a friendly game of beach football.

Monaco
Las Vegas casinos are so passé. If you want to find out how the world's super-elite get their gambling kicks, you need to head for the roulette tables of Monaco. To really show off, arrive by yacht.

Sydney
You'll never be down Down Under. And Sydney, with its great bars, beaches and sports events is the perfect place to hang out.

Jamaica
With so many great beach resorts dotted across the Caribbean, choosing one for your bucket list is tricky. But when it comes to partying, Jamaica seems to have the lot.

Ibiza
Its reputation as the party island of the Med is well deserved. If you plan to dance and expand your minds all night long, then you'll find plenty of unforgettable nightclubs here to do it in.

Antarctica
Fancy a little ocean cruise? Why not head for the one continent none of your party will have ever been to before? You'll certainly never run out of ice for your cocktails. The trouble is, the only naked chicks you'll see will be baby penguins.

Space
No joke this one. Several space travel companies offer paid-for flights into orbit. One of them – Space Adventures – is even planning future circumlunar missions. Be prepared to shell out several million pounds each for the privilege, however.

CHOOSING DAYTIME ACTIVITIES

Get 15 young men on a weekend away from their wives and girlfriends, and there's a strong temptation to hit the bottle at the first opportunity. A word of advice for you: don't. Your friends may egg you on but you won't be remembered as a good best man if you allow the groom to get absolutely plastered and pass out before the sun's even gone down. For this reason, you need to organise at minimum of one daytime activity that involves everyone in the stag party.

It's always a good idea to keep the exact details of what you're planning secret from the groom – the element of surprise adds a fun bit of nervous tension. You can give him a vague idea so that he brings along the correct footwear and clothing, but there's no need to give the game away.

Group activities always work better than individual ones. After all, the main purpose of the stag party is to allow all the groom's friends to get to know each other. And that can be hard if you're racing solo all afternoon in go-karts.

But bear in mind some of the different personalities coming on the party – skydiving or a jungle survival weekend in Sierra Leone may not be to everyone's taste. Plus there's the severe risk of broken bones to consider.

Playing sport

A welcome addition to any stag weekend is the injection of a bit of competition into the party activities. Get a large group of men together and even a game of tiddlywinks can turn into something as tense and competitive as the Olympic 100m final. You might want to split the group into two teams, perhaps with the groom as one captain and you, the best man, as the other. A five-a-side football match or a game of baseball will really get the competitive juices flowing and help the group bond. Plus it's easy to organise. Golf is always a great choice, since it doesn't exclude any unfit members of the group. There's no point demanding too much exertion on a stag party – no one will thank you for organising a 4 x 400m relay race, particularly if it is on Saturday morning when you have spent all of Friday night out on the town.

And what about having a special trophy made for the winning team? You could get the details of the stag party engraved on it beforehand.

Here are a few sports you can play:

Football: Five-a-side football means no one will have to sprint at full-pelt down the wing. The smaller pitch and less vigorous tackling will also help keep injuries down.

Cricket: A good choice for the lazier guys in the group. A limited overs game is a great way to spend an afternoon.

Ten-pin Bowling: Book several adjacent lanes to keep the group together. An extra bonus is that you can drink during play.

Darts: Another drink-friendly sport but one that requires maths skills and the throwing of sharp weapons. Uh-oh.

Fishing: There's nothing like being on a small boat to help a bunch of guys bond. Make sure you pack the seasick pills and that the groom gets to catch a whopper.

Paintballing: Separate the party into two teams and shoot the hell out of each other. Finish the day with a game of 'Everyone hunt the groom'!

Golf: This is by far the most popular stag party sport, since you can handicap the different levels of play, and you can include the fat and the unfit. Here's a hint: tell the golf club it's a business trip rather than a stag party. And keep the hip flasks hidden until you're out of sight of the clubhouse. Groundsmen will rightly protect their greens to the death.

Here are a few suggestions for different golf competitions you can play:

Stableford: This is perfect for weaker golfers, since the scoring system is so forgiving. Rather than counting every stroke in your entire round, you are given points according to the number of strokes you take on each hole. Complete the hole four strokes under par and you score six points; three strokes under par and you score five points; two strokes under gives you four points; one stroke under and it's three points; equal par and you score two points; one stroke over par and it's one point; anything else and you score zero. The winner is the player with the highest points total at the end of the round.

Skins: Nothing like a bit of gambling to liven up a stag party and bring out the competitive side in people. In a skins game, the winner of each hole gets to take cash off his fellow players. Set the prize money for each hole in advance. If you tie on a hole, the prize money is carried over to the next hole.

Nine points: In this version, each hole is worth nine points. The player who completes the hole in the fewest strokes wins five points; the runner-up wins three points; and third place gets just one

point. No points for fourth place or beyond. Should two players tie for first place, they receive four points each. If all three players tie, it's three points each. There are also bonus points: shoot a birdie and you get an extra two points, while an eagle wins you an extra three points.

Speed golf: Some golfers are very skilled, but they're possibly a bit tubby round the middle. Here's your chance to get your own back on them. In speed golf, you count both the number of strokes and the length of time it takes to complete a round. So players run between shots and carry as few clubs as possible. The overall score is arrived at by adding the number of minutes to the total number of strokes. If the groom is a bit of a petrol head, you could hire

Real-life groom

Golf has been the focus of many a great stag party. Not long ago, in South Africa, one bull party – as they call it there – hired out a golf club for the whole day. Proceedings started with a boozy lunch in the clubhouse. Afterwards, when everyone was fully fuelled, the best man split them up into three groups of four and let everyone loose on the course for a game of Scramble. But at the end of each hole there was a little surprise: following them round the course were two lovely ladies in a golf buggy, equipped with its very own mobile bar. After negotiating each green, the golfers were offered the drink of their choice by the two barwomen. Needless to say, said women were dressed in nothing more than revealing bikinis.

golf buggies to drive between each shot rather than run.

Scramble: On a stag do, you're bound to have that rather embarrassing situation where several of the players can't play for toffee. In this version, you don't have to worry about that, since stronger players carry the weaker ones.

Each player in the team tees off as normal. The team then democratically decides whose shot was best, ignoring the other shots. Players play their second shot from within a club's length of where the best first shot lies; their third shot from within a club's length of where the best second shot lies; and so on until the hole is completed. To score, you add up the total number of best shots required to complete the hole.

Bingo bango bongo: This version rewards consistent play. On each hole, there are three ways to earn a point: the first player to get his ball on the green (bingo); the closest to the hole once everyone is on the green (bango); or the first in the hole (bongo). The lowest overall score on each hole also wins an extra two points. At the end of the round, add up all the points to find out who is the winner.

Watching sport

Perhaps competing in sport is a little too rigorous. Why not spectate instead? You may encounter a few problems trying to procure a dozen tickets for Manchester United or Chelsea, however, so don't be disappointed if you fail to get pitch-side seats on the halfway line for the big game. You may have to set your sights a bit lower, especially if you all want to sit together.

Failing that, you could spend a day at the races or a night at the dog track. Even if the party members have no interest in racing, the gambling element will soon get everyone cheering along. You could even start a gambling kitty where everyone chips in a bit of cash and the groom gets to choose which horse to put it on. You can guarantee any winnings will all get blown on the final race of the day.

Another option is to book an area at a sports bar when a major sporting event is taking place and watch it on the big screen instead. That way you get to enjoy the game and you have easy access to beers, food and an excellent view. And if there are a decent number of you watching the screen, you can guarantee there will be a great atmosphere, too.

Festival time

Why not coincide the stag weekend with one of the world's famous festivals? That way, not only will the stag have the time of his life but you'll be remembered as a legendary party organiser.

Running of the Bulls, Pamplona, Spain (July): If running through narrow streets pursued by sharp-horned angry beasts doesn't prepare the groom for married life, then there's a good chance nothing will. Just don't let him get gored or his future bride will never forgive you.

Oktoberfest, Munich, Germany (October): Beer, beer and more beer. Plus plenty of lederhosen, buxom young Frauleins and lots of singing. Did we mention the beer?

Summerfest, Milwaukee, USA (June and July): With between 800,000 and one million spectators, this is the biggest music festival in the world. Make sure you don't lose the groom in the crowd.

La Tomatina, Bunol, Spain (August): This is essentially one massive food fight with over 150,000 tomatoes flying through the air. The perfect baptism for the groom before he embarks on married life.

Carnival of Venice, Italy (February): With three million visitors, gorgeous outfits and stunning masks, you could have some fun dressing everyone up for this one. Save the most outrageous costume for the groom.

Calgary Stampede, Calgary, Canada (July): This event is the ultimate cowboy festival, featuring rodeos, wrangling and wagon racing. Why not dress the groom in a cowboy hat, chaps and a sheriff's badge? And give him a hobby horse to ride while you're at it.

South by Southwest, Austin, USA (March): Staged at around 90 venues across the capital of Texas, this is one of the coolest music festivals in North America. Try to get the groom up on one of the stages.

The kitty system

One of the biggest headaches of a stag party is paying for all the drinks. With so many different bars to visit and cocktails to sample, you're never going to find a completely fair way to share out the cost of the rounds.

There is one solution, however: the kitty system. At the beginning of the evening, ask everyone to contribute a set amount towards buying the drinks; the groom is the only exception, as everyone else chips in for him. Place all the cash in one large wallet which you then designate 'the kitty'. From then on, all drinks are bought from kitty money. But don't worry, this doesn't mean that you, as best man, will end up spending the whole evening queuing for drinks. You can send anyone up to the bar with the kitty without having to

Rio Carnival, Rio de Janeiro, Brazil (February): With around two million people on the streets every day, this is possibly the biggest carnival in the world. You're sure to see some crazy, weird and wonderful sights.

worry about who has previously paid for a round and who hasn't.

Try to inject the kitty with enough cash to last all night. You'll find it's far easier to persuade everyone in the party to part with one large amount of cash at  the beginning of the evening rather than going back again and again begging for further contributions.

What if you have a mix of slow and fast drinkers? The groom's university friends are undoubtedly going to sink the beers a lot faster than his friends from accounts. One way round this problem is to operate two kitty systems – one for the big boozers and one for the lightweights.

CHOOSING EVENING ACTIVITIES

Once the sun goes down, it can be a lot harder to keep the troops together in one location. Imagine you're all out in the city centre where there are dozens of bars and clubs open for business. If you're not careful, you'll lose party members by the wayside and fail in your main task as best man: keeping the group together.

You have to formulate a plan in advance and get everyone to agree to it. Perhaps book a restaurant first so that everyone's initially around the same table. When it comes to drinking, do a bit of research before you go and try to find places that welcome large groups of lads and ideally will allow you to pre-book a few tables for your group. If you do decide to head off on a pub crawl later, make sure to keep the number of stops to a minimum, and the distances between bars very short. That way any stragglers will easily catch up.

And as obvious as it may sound, it's a good idea to punch everyone's phone number into your mobile before heading out for the evening.

Strip clubs: You know that old adage, 'What goes on tour, stays on tour'? It's complete rubbish. Should you all head for a strip joint, the bride will find out sooner or later. And you, as best man, will be the one most likely to carry the blame. Saying that, female nudity has been part of stag party celebrations since time immemorial, so it would be a mighty shame to break with tradition. If the bride-to-be is not the jealous type, then go right ahead and have a good time. If she is, you need to tread very carefully – Bridezilla won't be happy. Just don't say you weren't warned.

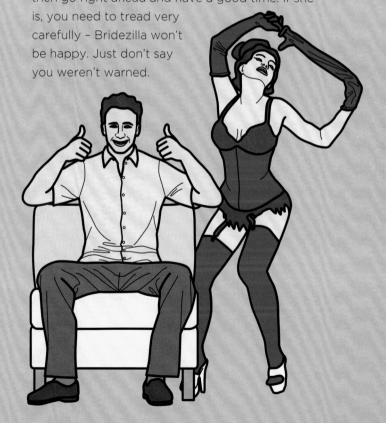

Stripper tips:
How to get out of a strip club with both your wallet and dignity intact

Door policy: Always be polite to the doormen, however many drinks you have inside you. They hold the ultimate power in a strip club.

Tip generously: Girls often have to pay a house fee to perform. If you're not willing to tip them, you'll get short shrift. Tip well and you'll get the best dances.

Be a gentleman: You wouldn't throw screwed-up fivers at a street busker. A topless dancer would be even more insulted.

No touchy feely: You need permission for all that stuff. And you rarely get it.

She's not a therapist: Eight drinks down and you may think she holds the answers to your love life/career/psychological problems but the truth is she doesn't, and she probably doesn't care. She's a dancer, not a shrink.

Don't try to pick up: However hot you think you are, remember these girls are professionals. And they've heard lines like 'Let me take you away from all this' a thousand times before. Don't ask for their phone numbers either.

Don't get frisky: Unless it's a very 'special' kind of strip club, any sexual advances will be firmly rebutted. There's a chance you may even get thrown out.

Never use a credit card: Can you imagine the trouble you'll be in if the bride finds a receipt from Spearmint Rhino in the groom's pocket?

Nightclubs: While a dozen boozy men strutting their stuff on the dance floor is no pretty sight, nightclubs can inject a bit of energy into a stag party. Just make sure you run it past the management before you all turn up at the door. There's nothing that upsets doormen more than a group of rowdy, drunken men all trying to squeeze their way in at the same time. If the bouncers look really inflexible, try splitting the party into groups of two or three and staggering your entry.

Casinos: The rules governing gambling differ enormously between different countries, and even between states in America. Always contact the casino in advance to check you'll get your party through the front door. You won't be a popular best man if you all turn up, pockets stuffed with cash, and no one even gets within sniffing distance of the gaming tables.

Choose a game that keeps the groom and his friends together on one table, such as roulette. With more solitary games, such as blackjack, you risk breaking up the party.

THE CULTURAL STAG PARTY

Say what? You mean it's possible to throw a great stag party that doesn't involve harems of strippers and lakes of booze? Surely not!

Although it sounds like a contradiction in terms, culturally enriching stag parties are becoming more and more popular. Unsurprisingly, as men get married later in life, the need to pickle oneself in alcohol and wake up face-down in a pool of vomit starts to lose its appeal somewhat.

Instead, many are opting for hiking weekends in the countryside, skiing trips, surfing trips, cooking weekends and festivals (see Festival time, page 38) among other more refined ideas. This may sound criminal to a group of twentysomethings hellbent on hitting the town, but for the older bachelor, a comparatively sedate weekend away with his oldest friends can be the perfect send-off before he embarks on married life.

Hiking: There's nothing like a long-distance hike to get everyone bonding together, but make sure that you tell the attendees to prepare for all weathers. Head out to the countryside and set yourselves a mission to walk 15 miles each day, staying at bed-and-breakfast accommodation along the way. You could even split the stag party into two groups, one led by the groom and one by you, the best man. Both groups have to meet up at a certain destination every evening, having used their orienteering skills to find the fastest route.

Skiing: Book a ski chalet for the weekend and aim to ski every run in the resort in record time. If you have skiers of different skill levels, you may want to split the group up into beginners, intermediate and advanced. Just make sure you all meet up for lunch and the après-ski.

Treasure hunt: Do a quick search online and you'll find lots of companies that organise treasure hunts – often spread out across an entire city. Most are aimed at corporate groups, but they will happily cater for stag parties, too. For those with a cultural bent, it can be a great way to get to know the architecture and backstory of a historical town.

Cooking course: Ideal for the gourmand groom. Find a cooking school willing to take on the whole stag party and fine-tune your culinary skills.

Arts course: The bride will never believe you if you tell her you've persuaded the groom and all his friends to spend the weekend practising their drawing and painting skills. But if your groom is a budding Van Gogh, why not?

Wilderness weekend: Sometimes the only way men can find their true inner selves is by going back to nature. Maybe you should hire a cabin in the middle of nowhere and see if you can all survive for 48 hours without any modern conveniences. Hint: take lots of tinned food.

CLOTHING THE GROOM AND THE USHERS

As best man, part of your job is to ensure the groom is subject to a little bit of humiliation. Whether it's gentle or full-blown is up to you. Only you know how much mental and physical anguish he is capable of enduring.

An outfit for the groom

First off you need to decide what he's going to wear all weekend. Floral-print dress, Superman costume, a Borat-style mankini, cowboy hat and chaps... the options are endless. And don't worry about going too far. This is your one chance to see your best friend strutting around as a transvestite. It shouldn't be missed. Besides, once he has a few beers inside him, any self-conscious feelings will quickly evaporate. At the end of a long boozy weekend, you may even find the groom has grown strangely attached to his new uniform.

Outfit ideas

Charity shops provide a wonderful array of cheap clothing. Head straight for the women's section and you may find that perfect oversized granny

dress and handbag combination. Don't worry if they clash – that's the whole idea. If you can find some high heels that fit, all the better.

Joke shops – both those on the high street and online – are essential, too. Stock up on comedy breasts, genitalia-themed headgear and the obligatory blow-up doll. Rude props may be highly immature, but they'll certainly liven up the party – and the photos.

Stag party T-shirts

As best man, it's not a bad idea to get T-shirts printed for every member of the stag party. On the back, you might display the name of each person. On the front, you can print the groom's name, the date and the party destination. It's a wise idea to opt for cheap T-shirts since you know there's going to be plenty of beer swilling about all weekend. It's perfectly OK to ask the other party members to reimburse you for the cost.

Practical jokes

Whatever you do, don't let the practical jokes get out of control. While it may be funny, even expected, to tie the groom to a lamp post in his underwear for a couple of hours (leave his underpants on or he'll get arrested!), you don't want him heading back home to his fiancée with his arm in a sling or his leg in a plaster cast. Likewise, shaving his eyebrows while he's asleep can be hilarious. But if they don't grow back before it's time to walk up the aisle, you're going to be a very unpopular best man indeed.

Rules on photography and social media

The groom's family – and especially his bride-to-be – won't want to see their beloved boy semi-naked, semi-conscious, and fully drunk. While it's great to take photos of the stag party activities during the day, once the booze starts flowing it's better to keep his reputation intact. Suggest to everyone that they put the cameras away once the sun goes down.

It may also be sensible to impose a social-media blackout over the course of a weekend. While you and the lads may find it funny to post pictures of the groom in a state, others back home definitely won't. If you have to share pictures, set up a WhatsApp group specifically for that purpose, rather than plaster incriminating images all over Facebook and Instagram.

STAG PARTY HORROR STORIES

With so much booze involved, and spirits naturally rather elevated, stag parties can quickly get out of hand. Not so bad if the party is in the groom's home town (provided he's not too unpopular with the local law, he should be able to sweet-talk himself out of a tricky situation), but what if you're heading further afield? What if it's grumpy Lithuanian policemen you run foul of?

Ultimately, it's the best man's job to keep the party in check. And with 15 rowdy stags to marshal, that can be a very big job.

Be sensitive to local laws. Yes, famous party towns (such as Las Vegas, Cancun and Daytona Beach in North America, or Prague, Barcelona and Tallin in Europe) are quite used to hosting groups of boozy young men but they still have local police keen to keep the peace. Party too hard and you could end up spending the night in a police cell. Not fun at the best of times; even less fun when you're sporting a dress and comedy breasts and sharing a cell with a tattooed murder suspect.

Real-life groom

A popular choice for many British stag parties is to head off to eastern European countries for the weekend, where the beer and strippers are plentiful. A few years ago, one such party arrived at an activity centre where they'd booked a paintballing session. Just as they arrived, however, a black, A-Team-style van suddenly skidded to a halt in front of them. Out jumped three thugs wearing ski masks and armed with guns. Quick as a flash, they bundled the groom into the back of the van and drove off at high speed into the woods.

The whole scenario was actually a practical joke arranged by the best man. The poor groom, however, thought he had been kidnapped for real and feared for his life. Desperate to escape his captors, he punched his way out of the van and leapt from the speeding vehicle onto the road. Result? A broken collar bone, an embarrassed best man and a very upset bride.

Practical jokes to avoid

However drunk you get, there are some lines you simply don't cross when it comes to practical jokes played on the groom.

Tattoos: Yes, how hilarious to get the groom so drunk that he agrees to getting 'Love' and 'Hate' inked across his knuckles. Not so hilarious when he has to walk down the aisle wearing gloves.

Close shaves: Legs, OK. At a push, partial pube-removal. But if you want the bride to ever speak to you again, stay clear of the head and the eyebrows.

Imprisonment: A night in the local slammer could be forgiven. You may even sweet-talk the local law into letting him off. But subject him to just five minutes in a South American or an Eastern European jail and he'll be crying for his mummy.

Public nudity: If you really want to chain him to a lamp post in Covent Garden or Trafalgar Square, then at least have the decency to leave him his underpants – although you could perhaps place them tantalizingly out of reach just for a laugh.

Drugging: He's going to expect a few lethal cocktails, but don't let him consume any drugs you wouldn't take yourself. Certainly not anything that will make him forget his own name.

Real-life groom

Back in the 1990s, a group of British army lads decided to celebrate their friend's impending nuptials with a camping trip in the mountains of Wales. Hiking, boozy barbecues, rude jokes around the campfire... it was all very active and wholesome. That is until the beer started talking and it was decided the groom needed the challenge of a night-time ramble. They drove him out to the middle of the Brecon Beacons in the pitch dark, stripped him down to his underpants and abandoned him to his own devices. The next day, after a full-on helicopter search, he was eventually found, battered, bruised and unconscious at the bottom of a mine shaft. On the plus side, at least his pants were still intact.

Celebrity stag parties

What goes on tour, stays on tour, right? Not always. Sometimes even the most guarded celebrities let slip details of their partying.

Prince Andrew: Future wife Fergie and Princess Diana played a trick on Prince Andrew the night of his stag party by dressing up as policewomen and surprising him as he returned home.

Wes Welker: the NFL star tried to gatecrash another party with his buddies while on his stag party. Security guards quickly waded in, restrained Welker and swiftly kicked him off the property.

Mario Lopez: The TV star told his future wife he was going marlin fishing. What he was actually doing was fishing for loose women. Two weeks after he got married, his wife found out and divorced him.

Jimmy Stewart: Before he got hitched in 1949, the star of It's a *Wonderful Life* took over a famous Hollywood restaurant. Part of the entertainment included a dwarf actor from *The Wizard of Oz* who was hired to put on a baby costume and urinate on the groom.

GETTING THE STAG HOME

In years to come, you might find yourself babysitting the groom's offspring. The stag party may give you a bit of practice for this role, except here you'll be looking after the groom himself.

Chances are by the end of the night he'll be in no fit state to stagger home or to the hotel on his own. It's your job to guide him back – even carry him, if necessary. No one's expecting you to remain sober. Certainly not. In fact, as best man, you've got to get the party started. But take it easy and remember that, ultimately, the groom is your responsibility.

When things go awry

Sometimes – God forbid – even the most meticulously planned stag party can go horribly wrong. Here are some tips on how to extricate yourself from hairy situations.

Police arrest: There are many ways you can end up on the wrong side of the law during a stag weekend. Be submissive, do what you're told and – especially if you're in a country with a teetering economy – have a lot of local dinero to bribe your way out of trouble. Avoid internal inspections if at all possible.

Severe drunkenness: It is almost certain this will affect the groom at some point over the weekend. The cure is simple: fresh air, strong coffee and a couple of curative buckets of water over the head. The following evening you can start all over again.

Ejection from a nightclub: Do not, on any account, try to remonstrate with a nightclub doorman. They love nothing more than forcefully ejecting drunk troublemakers from their establishment. Should said troublemaker be the groom, it's your job as best man to round up the troops and loyally follow him out.

Injury to groom: Asking people to take part in an unfamiliar activity, such as mountain biking, rock climbing or downing 10 shots of sambuca, means that even on the tamest of stag weekends there is the chance that someone will get hurt, and it's often the groom. No matter who or what caused the injury, you can guarantee the bride will pin the blame on you. So the most important thing is to disguise the wound. If he breaks an arm, you want to make sure the plaster cast fits snugly inside the arm of his wedding suit jacket. If he burns his eyebrows off, get hold of some fake ones that he can wear on the big day. If he finds himself with two black eyes, come the morning of the wedding it will be you applying the make-up.

Regretted tattoos: At midnight, with two bottles of Jack Daniels inside you, it can all seem quite normal to have a naked lady, a python and a dagger tattooed on your belly. But in the cold, grey light of dawn... Head immediately for a tattoo removal specialist. It can take a number of sessions over the course of several weeks to fully remove a tattoo, so best get started straight away.

PART 2

WEDDING REHEARSAL AND DINNER

A FAMILY AFFAIR

As best man, a crucial part of your role is to keep the bride and her family sweet at all times. Don't worry too much about the groom – he'll forgive a few mishaps along the way. But whatever you do, do NOT underestimate the importance of the bride-to-be and the in-laws.

Whether you've met the bride's parents before or not, you have to be cool, calm and collected in all dealings with them. Perhaps give them a call in the months leading up to the wedding to reassure them that you're fully prepared to carry out your best-man duties and will do everything you can to make sure their daughter's special day goes according to plan. The bride's father could well be remortgaging his house to pay for the wedding, so chances are he'll be a little concerned at the prospect of the best man getting the groom drunk as a lord the night before the main event, or delivering an idiotic speech on the big day.

THE WEDDING REHEARSAL

This is the first opportunity you'll get to really shine, and with so many important members of the wedding party in attendance, you'd better shine brightly.

The rehearsal is normally a fairly straightforward process: you all turn up at the wedding venue – smartly dressed, but not in wedding gear – and act out a dry run of the ceremony. Depending on the bride and groom's religion (or lack thereof), the wedding official will be leading proceedings. Reassure them and everyone else in the wedding party that you have all your responsibilities – including all the ushers – well under control. No one wants this wedding to end up on one of those awful home video comedy shows (you know the type – where the bride trips on her dress and falls in a pond, or the groom vomits in the church aisle).

Pecking order

There's a strict pecking order among the many members of the wedding party. By far the most important person is the bride, with her mother coming a few rungs below her. Then comes the bride's father who, more often than not, has made the most significant financial outlay. Below him is the groom, followed by the maid of honour. Bottom of the heap is you, the best man. Given your lowly position, it's a good idea to keep quiet during the rehearsal. Apart from the guidance you offer all the ushers, now isn't the time to make changes to the ceremony. Your views on the minister's dandruff or the choice of music won't be welcome, so just go with the flow.

Wedding rehearsal tips:

- Make a mental note of the running order of the ceremony.

- Find out where the wedding party and guests are supposed to sit.

- Brief all the groomsmen on their duties.

- Establish where you and the groom should stand at the start of the ceremony.

- Find out where the toilets are – you'll be asked the location many times on the day.

THE REHEARSAL DINNER

This is a key feature of most American weddings, partly because so many family members and guests travel such long distances to be there, but it's becoming increasingly common in the UK, too.

Traditionally, the rehearsal dinner is hosted by the parents of the groom, which is fair enough bearing in mind the bride's parents already have enough to worry about and pay for with the wedding itself. Depending on the families involved, the dinner can be a very casual affair or something quite formal, but the groom's family won't want people thinking that they're trying to upstage the main event the following day. For that reason, it's likely to fall towards the more casual end of the spectrum.

Be prepared to meet a lot of old friends and relatives. With so many guests coming from out of town (it's amazing how far people will travel for a free dinner and a few glasses of champagne), you may find yourself sandwiched between a dotty old aunt and someone's bored teenage daughter. Fortunately, all the attention will be on the bride and groom but, as best man, you've got to be on your best behaviour.

There's a chance you may get called upon to offer up a few words. Don't worry, it really is only a few words. Save all your energy and your best material for your 15 minutes of fame the following day. If you do get asked to speak, keep it simple, thank everyone for coming and wax lyrical about how excited you all are about what's to come.

PART 3

WRITING
THE SPEECH

BE PREPARED

We all procrastinate. It's human nature. But if you want to be sure of performing well when you deliver your speech, you need to start preparing it at least a month before the big day – preferably longer if you can. Remember, you'll be busy enough as it is with all your stag party and rehearsal dinner duties.

Do not for a minute imagine you can bash out a few hundred words on your phone during the journey home from work the night before or, even worse, simply wing it on the day of the wedding. You haven't been appointed to mumble a few kind words and propose a quick toast. Oh no. Face the facts – you are very much the main act (albeit an unpaid one). The groom, the bride and her entire family are all counting on you to perform, and while you don't need to be in the same oratorical league as Martin Luther King or John F. Kennedy, you do need to look like you've made an effort. And, unfortunately, even for the most skilled charmer, that requires some preparation.

BASIC SPEECH STRUCTURE

There's nothing particularly complicated about structuring your speech. Long gone are the days when you were expected to adhere to a strict formula. These days the best man's speech should have more of a personal touch, and if that means straying from the more traditional aspects, then so be it.

Saying that, it's a good idea to give yourself a checklist of basic elements you need to include. During the speech your audience will be listening out for key milestones where they can expect to laugh, applaud and cheer.

Your 10-point speech checklist:

1. A great opening line

Like all great public speakers – politicians, comedians, army generals, team captains, CEOs – you need to get your audience on side right from the very beginning. Ideally, you want to kick off with an opening line that gets everyone laughing or cheering (see page 80).

Finding a balance

It can be tricky gauging how far you can go when it comes to mocking or complimenting the groom, and, as his best friend, only you will know the limit. Ridicule him too much and you will appear cruel; compliment him too whole-heartedly and you may find your audience reaching for the sick bags. One way round this dilemma – and a method that works well with an often slightly cynical Anglo-Saxon audience – is to intersperse the compliments with ridicule. So, after you've told everyone about the time he saved a puppy from drowning, you could also drop in the anecdote about how he used to pull the wings off flies. Or once you've reminded the guests of how he graduated from university with flying colours, you could also tell them that he's got the common sense of a gnat.

2. Acknowledge previous speakers

As best man, you will usually be the last to deliver a speech – the main act, so to speak. As such, it's vital that you thank the groom, the father of the bride and anyone else who may have spoken before you, regardless of the quality. The bride's father may have bored the pants off the entire room but you nevertheless must applaud his efforts with as much sincerity as you can muster.

3. Thank the wedding couple on behalf of the bridesmaids

In the past, one of the traditional functions of the best man's speech was to thank the bride and groom for the presents they had given the bridesmaids. Provided the maid of honour isn't delivering her own speech (at some weddings she will), this can be a nice touch, and a nod to tradition. To really get into everyone's good books, you could even add a few compliments about how wonderful all the bridesmaids look.

4. Congratulate the newlyweds

Congratulations for the happy couple will be coming thick and fast from just about everyone in the room and you must be no exception. The trick is not to make it sound too cheesy.

5. Compliment the bride

Again, the whole party will already have done this ad infinitum, but that doesn't mean you're absolved of this duty. Even though it's for the groom to wax lyrical about the charms of his bride, everyone else (including her) will be expecting a few compliments from the best man, too. You can cleverly turn it to your own benefit, however. If you find your speech starts to flag or your audience is beginning to get distracted, throw in a line about how beautiful the bride looks and you're guaranteed a cheer from the entire room.

6. Mock the groom

Now comes the fun part – the bit where you get to ridicule your best friend with impunity. Even better is the fact that he can't retaliate because he's already delivered his speech and you're now in charge of the microphone. Wedding guests will be looking forward to this part of the speech, and for many of them it will be a chance to laugh at the groom's innermost secrets and funniest faults. You can be pretty merciless (within reason), just make sure you don't assassinate his character too cruelly, or overstep the line and utterly humiliate him (see page 84).

7. The serious bit

However much you enjoy mocking your best friend, you've got to be a little bit emotional, too. As his best man, you have to prove that he's a worthy husband for the bride. That means providing evidence of what an upstanding chap he is at heart, and what a loyal friend he's been to you all these years. Chuck in a line here about how lucky the bride and groom are to have found each other.

Speech order and length

At traditional weddings, there are three speeches. First up is the father of the bride, then the groom, then your good self, the best man. But nowadays it's more and more common for other members of the wedding party to speak. Perhaps the bride will ask her godfather to entertain the guests. There may be two best men, each of whom gives a speech. It's even possible that the maid of honour, a stepfather or even the bride herself will want to take to the floor. Whatever the running order, the best man should always come last. He is the main act.

How long should you speak for? That, of course, depends on the occasion. Should your best friend be marrying the Prime Minister's daughter at a Downing Street reception, you'd be expected to pull out all the stops and give the guests a good half an hour. But if it's a quick ceremony at the Elvis Presley Chapel in Las Vegas, you could probably get away with three minutes. If you don't already know

the demographic make-up of your audience – and
for how long they're likely to pay attention – ask the
groom to provide some guidance. But, as a general
rule, the best man's speech should last the longest
of all the speeches, ideally somewhere between
10 and 15 minutes.

8. Absent friends

There are always a few guests who can't make it to the wedding. In the old days, you would read out congratulatory telegrams from them. Nowadays, it's more likely to be emails. If there aren't many to read out, you could always fabricate some funny ones (see page 88).

9. Quotes and poems

There's nothing like a proper writer to lend your speech a certain gravitas. Just make sure you choose the appropriate words. Shakespeare or Hemingway are always a good call. Not so good are *Mein Kampf* or *Playboy* magazine. Aim to be poignant but amusing (see page 90).

10. The toast

Always wrap up your speech with a heartfelt toast to the bride and groom (see page 98). Make sure to give the guests a few seconds' warning before you ask them to stand so they have time to top up their glasses.

WRITING IT DOWN

If you're not used to writing, this can seem like a daunting task. Depending on your job, it may be years since you put more than a few hundred words down on paper. Worry not. Use the basic speech structure on page 70 as your guide and jot down bullet points next to each of the 10 items on the checklist. Once you've done this, you will have the confidence to flesh out these bullet points at a later date. Type up your initial notes on your computer. It should be a work in progress, one that you add to and hone in the weeks leading up to the wedding. You can fine-tune it to perfection right up to the big day itself.

Printing out the speech

Flashier best men may opt to memorise their entire speech and deliver it on the day without any prompting. For most mere mortals (with full-time jobs) this simply isn't possible. On the other hand, it's not always wise to print out the speech verbatim because you will risk it sounding a little stilted on delivery. Instead, it's much better to do what many professional speakers – including world leaders – do: write down the bullet points of your speech on cue cards. This means you won't forget any of the anecdotes or the running order of the speech but you'll sound much more natural when you take to the floor.

Whether or not you use bullet points or the speech in its entirety, you need to think about the kind of paper you print your speech out on. Thin sheets of the standard paper you use for your home printer will flap about in your hands (especially if you're a bit nervous) and distract the guests. Smaller pieces of thick card, however, will sit comfortably in one hand without fluttering and are more discreet.

OPENING LINES

It doesn't need to be pant-wettingly funny, nor entirely original (none of the ones listed here are), but it's always good to begin your speech with a few lines that should elicit either a hearty laugh or a round of applause.

Remember that you don't need the comedic skills of Steve Martin or Billy Connolly. Your audience hasn't paid to be there, and everyone will be keen to give you a warm reception. Something vaguely witty will suffice. And if comedy really isn't your strong point, why not be upbeat instead? Simply point out what a beautiful couple the newlyweds make. Instead of a laugh, you'll get a rousing cheer – which will give you an equally strong boost of confidence as you begin your speech.

10 wonderful opening lines:

❝ We had a bit of trouble today working out who was going to sit at which table. To keep things fair, we decided to reward the guests who spent the most on wedding gifts by seating them near the front. Everyone else is seated behind them in decreasing order of gift value. So, to those of you

right at the back in the cheap seats: if you can hear me, on behalf of the bride and groom, thanks very much for the beautiful corkscrew.**"**

"Typical. Gallons and gallons of free champagne, and I'm last to make a speech, which means I haven't tasted a single drop yet.**"**

"Good afternoon, ladies and gentlemen. I am the best man. My name is John-what-would-you-like-to-drink?**"**

" What more can you say about a man who is handsome, intelligent, popular and courageous? Anyway, that's enough about me. The real reason I'm here is to talk about the groom. **"**

" That was a truly lovely speech you made just now, [groom]. You should make the most of it. Now that you're married, it will be the last time you get to speak for more than two minutes without being interrupted. **"**

" Earlier today [the bride] gave me strict instructions on the rude and embarrassing stories about [the groom] that I wasn't allowed to reveal to you all. [Remove a pile of cue cards from your hand and throw them onto the floor beside you.] OK, what do I have left, then? Not much, I can tell you. **"**

" We have a very close relationship, [the groom] and I. I've been like a mother to him over the years. I've helped him drink from the bottle. I've seen him crawl across the carpet in just his underpants. There have been many times when I've had to help him get dressed. Unfortunately, I've also regularly had to clean up when he's been sick or soiled himself. **"**

"Some of you may have noticed a bit of money exchanging hands before I started my speech. Apparently, there's a bet on about how long my speech is going to be. I even had a little wager myself, and backed myself at just over two hours. With over £500 up for grabs, you may as well sit back, make yourselves comfortable and be ready for a very long evening."

"I'd like to start off by saying how utterly stunning the bride looks today. As for [the groom]. Well, we tried our best."

"Many thanks to the minister at today's wedding ceremony. What a lovely guy. When [the bride] told him she was so nervous that she was worried she'd forget what she was supposed to do, he immediately reassured her. He told her she needed to remember just three things: AISLE, because that was what she had to walk along. ALTAR, because that was where she would get married. And HYMN, because that's what she would sing afterwards. I spotted her, just before she came into the church. She was taking the minister's advice quite seriously because I heard her repeating the words 'AISLE, ALTAR, HYMN! AISLE, ALTAR, HYMN! AISLE, ALTAR, HYMN!'"

MOCKING THE GROOM

A major part of your speech should focus on funny stories about the groom. While you want to regale the audience – and gently mock the groom – you shouldn't assassinate his character too much. That should have been done during the stag party. What you're after is anecdotes that help to portray the quirkier side of his character; don't dig the dirt so deep that his bride ends up wishing she hadn't married him.

It's possible you've known the groom for years. Think back to when you were kids, or your college days. Maybe you used to work with him? Surely you can unearth some great stories from crazy nights you've spent together. What about weird hobbies, bad taste in music, fashion disasters, awful haircuts? All ripe material for your speech.

Family and friends

The groom's friends, family and workmates can be a great source of funny anecdotes. Send some emails fishing for embarrassing stories before you begin writing the speech. Ask his siblings what he was like as a little boy. Maybe his parents kept all his old school reports. His work colleagues will no doubt love to expose his professional shortcomings. If you're struggling for material, don't be afraid to exaggerate. Never let the facts get in the way of a good story.

Photographic evidence

It'll be even better if you can get hold of some old photos of the groom when he was not looking his finest. His family will have plenty of material. Ask school friends to dig out his worst haircuts and clothing choices. Depending on the hardware, you could project these photos onto a screen during your speech or display them on the walls of the venue for all to see.

Subjects to avoid

Of course you want to embarrass the groom. By all means make him squirm in his seat. But you don't want him wishing the ground beneath him would swallow him up. Some subjects are a definite no-no. His parents, relatives, in-laws and possibly work colleagues are all in attendance. They don't need to know, for example, about his raging syphilis. Besides, you should have exposed all the rude stuff at the stag party. If in doubt, leave it out.

Ex-girlfriends: The last thing the bride wants to hear on her wedding day is details of her new husband's past conquests.

Ex-wives: There's a chance the bride or groom has been married before. Now is not the time to remind everyone.

Adult jokes: There's nothing wrong with a few innuendoes or cheeky humour, but don't go too far. There will be grannies and children in your audience, and possibly the minister who presided over the ceremony. Don't be crass.

Drink, drugs, gambling: Hopefully, the only thing he'll be addicted to from this day forth is love for his wife.

Politically incorrect jokes: This is a lovely wedding with shiny, happy people in attendance. It's not a convention for the KKK.

The in-laws: Mother-in-law jokes have provided comedians with material for decades, but a room filled with the mother- of-the-bride's family and friends is not the best time to try out your own material – unless, of course, you fancy a run-in with her furious husband.

MESSAGES FROM ABSENT FRIENDS

Every wedding has the odd absentee. A bed-bound granny, perhaps, who's one sandwich short of a picnic. Or an old friend now living on the other side of the world. One of the best man's traditional roles is to read out messages from these absentees. The bride and groom will tell you if there are some to be read out. Years ago these would have been in the form of a telegram.

While you obviously need to read out the messages with respect, there's a great opportunity to get a laugh from your audience. Once you've relayed the genuine messages, why not throw in a rogue one?

❝ Here's a message from the groom's football team. Unfortunately, none of them could attend today because they're competing in their league cup final. But they wanted to offer their congratulations to [the groom] and [the bride]. And they said [the bride] ought to know that this season [the groom] has been utterly useless in every position. They all hope she has a bit more luck tonight.❞

Or:

❝ A message from Auntie Flo all the way down under in Australia. She says: 'Congratulations. Please could you send me a photo of the bride and groom... mounted.'**❞**

Or:

❝ Dear [groom]. Congratulations to both you and your bride on this very happy day. By the way, do you wish to renew your subscription?

Yours truly, *Hustler* magazine**❞**

QUOTES AND POEMS

Professional writers always say it best. Whether you're trying to describe the groom's character or his relationship with his new wife, a great poem or quote can do the job perfectly. Make sure your chosen passage is succinct, though. Read out *Paradise Lost* in its entirety and you'll lose 95 percent of your audience.

A quotation or poem normally signals to the guests that you're starting to wrap up your speech. Since you're the final speech of the day,

they may already have sat patiently through 45 minutes of speaking. And their bladders will undoubtedly be full of champagne.

Finally, keep your quotes and poems tasteful and appropriate. This is hardly the time or place for an epigram from Adolf Hitler.

Great quotations for a best man's speech

Serious ones:

❝ When marrying, ask yourself this question: Do you believe that you will be able to converse well with this person into your old age? Everything else in marriage is transitory. ❞

– Friedrich Nietzsche

❝ Let the wife make the husband glad to come home, and let him make her sorry to see him leave. ❞

– Martin Luther

❝ One should believe in marriage as in the immortality of the soul. ❞

– Honoré de Balzac

❝ If there is such a thing as a good marriage, it is because it resembles friendship rather than love. ❞

– Michel de Montaigne

❝Marrying for love may be a bit risky, but it is so honest that God can't help but smile on it.**❞**

– **Josh Billings**

❝A journey is like marriage. The certain way to be wrong is to think you control it.**❞**

– **John Steinbeck**

❝Happy is the man who finds a true friend, and far happier is he who finds that true friend in his wife.**❞**

– **Franz Schubert**

❝Don't marry the person you think you can live with; marry only the individual you think you can't live without.**❞**

– **James C. Dobson**

❝Marriage should be a duet – when one sings, the other claps.**❞**

– **Joe Murray**

❝I have found the paradox: that if you love until it hurts, there can be no more hurt, only more love.**❞**

– **Mother Teresa**

❝ Keep love in your heart. A life without it is like a sunless garden when the flowers are dead. **❞**

– Oscar Wilde

❝ The best thing to hold onto in life is each other. **❞**

– Audrey Hepburn

❝ Everything is clearer when you're in love. **❞**

– John Lennon

❝ Love is like a friendship caught on fire. In the beginning a flame, very pretty, often hot and fierce, but still only light and flickering. As love grows older, our hearts mature and our love becomes as coals – deep-burning and unquenchable. **❞**

– Bruce Lee

❝ Love is composed of a single soul inhabiting two bodies. **❞**

– Aristotle

❝ We are all born for love. It is the principle of existence, and its only end. **❞**

– Benjamin Disraeli

❝ To love and be loved is to feel the sun from both sides. **❞**

– David Viscott

❝Love is everything it's cracked up to be. It really is worth fighting for, being brave for, risking everything for.**❞**

– **Erica Jong**

❝One word frees us of all the weight and pain of life: that word is love.**❞**

– **Sophocles**

Irreverent ones:

❝I have learned that only two things are necessary to keep one's wife happy. First, let her think she's having her own way. And second, let her have it.**❞**

– **Lyndon B. Johnson**

❝Men who have a pierced ear are better prepared for marriage – they've experienced pain and bought jewellery.**❞**

– **Rita Rudner**

❝Marriage is the alliance of two people, one of whom never remembers birthdays and the other who never forgets them.**❞**

– **Ogden Nash**

❝Marriage – as its veterans know well – is the continuous process of getting used to things you hadn't expected.**❞**

– **Tom Mullen**

❝After seven years of marriage, I'm sure of two things. First, never wallpaper together, and second, you'll need two bathrooms – both for her. The rest is a mystery, but a mystery I love to be involved in.**❞**

– Dennis Miller

❝An occasional lucky guess as to what makes a wife tick is the best a man can hope for. Even then, no sooner has he learned how to cope with the tick than she tocks.**❞**

– Ogden Nash

❝I love being married. It's so great to find that one special person you want to annoy for the rest of your life.**❞**

– Rita Rudner

❝Marriage is a wonderful invention: then again, so is a bicycle repair kit.**❞**

– Billy Connolly

❝Marriage resembles a pair of shears, so joined that they cannot be separated; often moving in opposite directions, yet always punishing those who come between them.**❞**

– Sydney Smith

Poems

There's an endless number of poems you might read from, and choosing one depends on your relationship with the groom, and his relationship with his new wife. Here are a few classics suitable for most weddings. Be warned, though: it's more appropriate for the groom to read out an entire poem during his speech. As best man, it would sound better (and less slushy) if you read out just a few key lines in dedication to the bride and groom. A quick search online will direct you to the poems in full.

The Owl and the Pussycat by Edward Lear
A Vow by Wendy Cope
Bridled Vows by Ian Duhig
Love Listen by Anne Gray
The Vows Moment Wobbles the Sonnet
    by David Hart
For a Wedding by Michael Longley
Sonnet 116 by William Shakespeare
Rings by Carol Ann Duffy
Nuptials by John Agard
Fidelity by D.H. Lawrence
Marriage Advice by Jane Wells
On Marriage by Kahlil Gibran
So, We'll Go No More a Roving
    by Lord Byron
Love and Friendship by Emily Brontë

Original poems

I f you fancy yourself as a modern-day Shakespeare, why not have a crack at writing a poem yourself? After all, you probably know the bride and groom better than anyone. A word of warning, though: don't be over-sentimental. You want wedding guests clapping, not gagging.

Otherwise you could think about hiring the services of a professional poet. Have a look online and you'll find plenty of writers willing to pen an original poem for your bride and groom. Be warned: prices and quality differ enormously.

THE TOAST

Congratulations. You've made it to the end of your speech without any mishaps. Just one final task awaits you: the toast.

Be sure to give the guests a few moments' notice so that they have time to charge their glasses. Then ask everyone to stand up.

There are hundreds of different wedding toasts you can choose from, some traditional, some irreverent, some downright cheesy. You'll know which style will work best. But whatever words you opt for, make sure you punctuate the toast with a rousing 'To the bride and groom!' or 'To the happy couple!', after which everyone will clink their glasses and take a drink. If you're delivering your speech while standing next to your dinner table, then you can raise your glass to the whole room when you want them

to drink. If you're up on stage, you can still propose a toast without a glass in your hand.

Great wedding toasts

"A toast to the beautiful bride.
A toast to the luckiest groom.
A toast to the person that tied.
A toast to you all in the room."

"May the roof above your heads
never fall in. And may you both
never fall out."

"To [the bride and groom]: May your marriage
be happy and long. May your children be
as gorgeous as you are. And may every
wedding speech you hear be shorter and
wittier than mine."

"May your love be added. May it never be
subtracted. May your household multiply.
May your hearts never be divided."

"To quote William Shakespeare from *Romeo
and Juliet*: 'May a flock of blessings alight upon
thy back.'"

"To quote William Shakespeare from
The Tempest: 'Look down, you gods,
and on this couple drop a blessed crown.'"

❝May 'for better or worse' be far better than worse.❞

❝May you live each day like your last and each night like your first.❞

❝May the most you ever wish for be the least you ever get.❞

❝Here's to your love, health, wealth. And, most importantly, the time to enjoy them.❞

❝May you grow old together on a single pillow.❞

❝May the best of your past be the worst of your future.❞

❝May all your ups and downs come only in the bedroom.❞

❝To keep your marriage brimming with love in the wedding cup, whenever you're wrong, admit it; whenever you're right, shut up.❞
    – Ogden Nash

PART 4

DELIVERING THE SPEECH

GETTING IT RIGHT

Speech delivery is just as important as speech content. Often more so. After all, you could write a speech worthy of Winston Churchill, but if you don't present it in a manner that engages and enthrals your audience, then it's all for nothing. It's unfortunate, but very true, that presentation often has more of an effect on an audience than content. You only have to watch certain celebrities speaking in public to realise that.

So why not glean a few tips from these celebrities? Television presenters, news readers, politicians and entertainers all try to imbue themselves with stage presence, using body language and eye contact, and changing the speed, pitch and tone of their delivery, all in an effort to attract and keep the attention of their audience.

The difference is that you're speaking at a friend's wedding, not at the MTV Music Awards or in the Houses of Parliament. You don't need the stage presence of Beyoncé or the Prime Minister. Your audience will be willing you to perform well. All you need to do is follow a few common-sense tips on public speaking.

Practising your speech

All great orators – from world leaders to stand-up comics – practise their speeches many times. And they're professionals, while you're a humble amateur – a very good one, of course, but an amateur all the same. Which means you need to practise until you're blue in the face.

Around 10 days to two weeks before the actual wedding, you should have committed a near-final version of your speech to paper. You'll be adding little details right up until the last moment, but the meat of what you plan to say will already be on the page.

Print it out, fold it up and stash it in your wallet. Any time you get a spare 10 minutes – on the train to work, during your lunch break, in the little boys' room – you should be reading it through and imagining yourself speaking at the wedding reception. And it's important, at least once every couple of days, that you give your speech a formal read-through. Use the following methods, but be sure to print the speech out on cue cards (see page 79).

Read to a mirror

Even if you aren't yet familiar with the speech content, you can hold the printed-out speech up in front of you while facing a body-length mirror and read it aloud to your own reflection. This way you can see your facial expressions and body language close-up. It also trains you to keep looking up at your audience – a crucial way of keeping their attention on the big day.

Film your speech

You don't need an expensive high-tech camera for this, a simple smart phone will suffice. Prop it up on a shelf in your living room, stand a few feet away and deliver your speech as if the phone were your audience.

   Now play the recording back. How does your stance appear? Are you standing up straight? Is your body language upbeat and positive? Do your hands keep straying into your pockets? Are you looking up regularly from your cue cards to your imaginary audience? What about the pace of your speech? There's often a tendency to rattle through it too quickly. Try to slow it down. Volume and enunciation are crucial, too. Really try to exaggerate the movements of your mouth so that, if there's no microphone on the actual wedding day, you will project your words to the very back of the room.

Read it to a friend

There's nothing like an honest second opinion. Ask someone you know well to be your practice audience. Rehearse your speech to them as if you were at the wedding itself. Glean some valuable and constructive advice on your performance. It sounds obvious, but your critic should be someone who's not attending the wedding with you. Otherwise you risk giving away all your best jokes. This process can also act as a handy check on the suitability of your jokes and anecdotes.

Dress rehearsal

It will feel a little odd at first, but you might consider practising your speech while wearing the suit you've chosen for the wedding. This will arm you with confidence and ensure you feel more natural on the actual wedding day, especially if you work in a job where suits or public speaking are rarely required.

Of course, there's a chance you and the groom haven't chosen your wedding suits by this stage. That's not a problem. Put on your best lounge suit instead. It's the feeling of standing up in formal wear and speaking aloud that you need to replicate.

DEALING WITH NERVES

There have been hundreds of surveys
conducted over the years trying to
discover what human beings fear the most.
Appearing regularly at the top of the list is
the idea of public speaking. In fact, there's
a good chance you bought this book for
the very reason that you suffer from this
phobia; it's actually a common condition,
known in medical circles as glossophobia.

Well, you can stop worrying right now. There are lots of clever little tips you can follow that will allay those nerves. Besides, as every great orator will tell you, a little bit of nervousness is good. That's what makes you perform well on the day. It's all about how you channel your anxiety. Don't let the nerves weigh you down and affect your speech delivery. Instead, you should turn all that nervousness into positive energy, giving yourself a physical and mental boost that then energises your audience. It takes practice but it works.

Don't let nerves get the better of you. Follow these basic tips.

Comfort break

It's never wise to embark on a 10-minute speech with a full bladder. A few minutes before the speeches start, pay a quick visit to the bathroom. Check your hair's in order, your tie's straight, there's no spinach caught between your teeth, no lipstick on your cheek...

Last-minute revision

After the wedding ceremony, and just before the wedding reception starts, it's a good idea to give yourself one last revision of your speech. Find a quiet corner and do a quick read-through of your words (in your head, not out loud) just to keep them fresh in your mind.

Psych yourself up

When it comes to building confidence, the final few seconds before you stand up to make your speech are often the most crucial. This is when you need to flood yourself with positive vibes. Breathe deeply in and out, right into your diaphragm – this will have a calming effect. You may be sweaty from nerves and your hot wedding suit, so wipe your brow with a

handkerchief. A good destressing exercise is to clench and unclench your fingers and toes repeatedly. While still seated, you can stretch out your neck and back.

Look at the guests

Remember that all the guests want you to perform well. You're not a smarmy politician nor a stand-up comic they've paid good money to see. You're the groom's best friend. All the wedding guests are totally on your side, willing you to shine.

Just before you stand up to speak, look around at their faces. Pick out people you know well, since it's much easier to speak to a group of friends than to strangers. Everyone will have had a couple of drinks by now. They are feeling happy and warm. They're really looking forward to your speech. They want to laugh when you tell them

Public-speaking courses

If you're really nervous about making your best man's speech, why not get some professional advice? Search online and you'll find plenty of companies offering tuition for public speaking. Some will even help you write your speech at the same time.

stories about the groom. They want to cheer when you point out the happy couple. Even if you make a few mistakes in your speech, they will happily let them pass. Don't forget that they are on your side. You'll never again have such an easy audience before you, so try to soak it up and enjoy every minute of it.

Think funny or happy

You're standing at the microphone, just about to deliver the opening lines of your speech. Everyone's looking at you. Normally you would be filled with dread. Right now it's time to use a psychological technique that tricks your brain into being confident instead of frightened. Think of something really happy or really funny. Perhaps someone told a hilarious joke at the stag party. Maybe you recall a time during your friendship with the groom when you were both at your happiest. As you remember this moment, your mind will relax, your body language will be positive, you will smile and any thoughts of anxiety will disappear. The guests will notice this positive aura around you and give you their full attention. Your speech will inevitably start off on a confident and positive note.

Hands

Hands in pockets? It all depends on the formality of the occasion. The Queen would not have been amused had Prince William's best man addressed the Royal Wedding with his hands stuffed deep in his trouser pockets. But for us mere mortals, there can be occasions during the speech where a discreet pocketing of the left hand might be appropriate. Perhaps when you're telling a joke, or while you're in full ridicule of the groom. Hands definitely out of pockets for the toast at the end of your speech, though.

Wet your mouth

Keep a glass of water next to you during your speech. You'll find that nerves and loud talking will make your mouth dry up. If there's no table nearby to rest the glass on, place it near your feet. No one will mind if you bend down every so often to take a sip. By keeping your mouth moist, you'll be able to enunciate your words much better.

Relish even the chuckles

Do not expect your guests to guffaw loudly at your jokes and funny stories. You are not Michael McIntyre. You are not Ricky Gervais. They will not be rolling around in the aisles, clutching their sides and crying with laughter. Even so, you are

Stance

You already look the cat's whiskers in your suit. Keep up this smart appearance by working on your stance during the speech. The way you stand has a massive impact on how the audience relates to your words.

Stand with your feet shoulder-width apart, one foot slightly in front of the other. Hold yourself upright with your shoulders back, your back straight and your chin level with the ground. Instead of locking your knees throughout the entire speech, every so often bend them slightly and rock forward a little onto the balls of your feet, as if you're ready to step forward. This will make you appear much more dynamic than if you stand back on your heels.

Look the part. Avoid these presentation no-nos.

1. Print out your speech on cue cards, not large sheets of paper, so it doesn't flap around in front of you.

2. Don't hide behind your speech. Alternate between looking up at your guests and down at your notes.

3. No slouching (see Stance, page 113). And no fiddling with coins in your pocket. Billiards is a game just for the stag party!

more than likely to get lots of chuckling. If the champagne has been flowing, perhaps even the odd belly laugh. Provided you have a large enough audience, even low-level laughing will sound impressive and should fill you with confidence. Feed off this confidence to deliver your speech with aplomb.

4. Adjust your tie before you take to the floor. You can loosen it later for the dancing.

5. Watch out for nervous tics that might distract your audience. Avoid constantly playing with your hair, straightening your tie or adjusting the ring on your finger.

6. Sniffing and coughing are not a good look. Blow your nose and clear your throat before you start the speech.

Don't apologise for nerves

You may be so nervous that you start to perspire, or your hands are a bit shaky. You may get tongue-tied on the odd line. Most guests – especially those sitting near the back – won't notice this. Even if they do, they will expect a few nerves. You certainly shouldn't apologise for being nervous, since this will make you focus on your lack of confidence rather than your speech.

Moving around

Many wedding reception venues will provide a microphone. If it's attached to a stand, you'll probably have to remain in the same position during the entire speech. But if at all possible, it's a great idea to relocate a couple of times – sometimes just by a few feet. Don't pace up and down like a prisoner on Death Row. Instead, at suitable points in your delivery, carry your mic to a different position and continue your speech from there. This will give other guests the chance to see you as you speak. Remain in the same spot and their view of you may be blocked by elaborate flower arrangements or supporting columns.

How to use a microphone

Some wedding reception venues provide their own PA systems. At others, it's up to the DJ to supply it. Whatever your case, make sure someone shows you how it works, well before the speeches start. You want to avoid that embarrassing situation where you're tapping the top of the mic and asking the people at the back of the room: 'Is this thing turned on?'

Check that you know where the on–off switch is. Learn how to take the mic on and off its stand without stumbling. When you're speaking, keep the mic near your mouth at all times – ideally about eight inches away.

ENUNCIATION

If the venue provides a microphone, you will have much less to worry about. Even the guests at the very back will hear what you've got to say.

But even with a microphone, you still will need to enunciate clearly in order to be understood by your audience. The key is to slightly exaggerate the movements of your mouth as you talk. Speak firmly and clearly; don't mumble. In casual conversation, many of us allow our sentences to fade out before the end. Obviously that's no good if you're making a speech. Each and every word should be distinguishable from the next. Remember, there are likely to be lots of old relatives in your audience. You want the grannies to appreciate your fine words rather than constantly fiddling with their hearing aids, don't you?

But what if there's no microphone? Or it's faulty? You're obviously going to have to speak much louder than normal. Aim your voice right to the back of the room. It's always tricky to know how much guests at the very back will be able to hear. Near the beginning of your speech, you should pick one or two of them out and ask them directly if you're speaking loud enough. If they can follow what you're saying, then you can guarantee everyone else will also be able to hear.

Dutch courage?

While there's nothing wrong with a glass of wine or champagne prior to your speech to calm your nerves, anything more and you're straying into dangerous territory. Quite often the wedding speeches come after the reception meal. You are likely to be third man up, which means everyone else will have had at least a few glasses when it's your turn to speak. Aside from the single glass, try not to imbibe. You will look very foolish indeed if you start slurring halfway through or lose your train of thought completely. Once you've finished speaking there's plenty of time to party and enjoy a few well-earned drinks.

TONE

When it comes to speeches, different weddings call for different styles of delivery. Perhaps your groom is marrying the daughter of a politician or minor royalty, in which case you'll obviously need to speak in a very formal manner. But for low-key wedding receptions at a normal hotel, you can afford to tone things down somewhat.

Saying that, you should always be yourself.
There's no point putting on false airs and graces.
You can talk naturally and still be formal and
respectful to the guests. Just be sure to cut
out the swearing – this isn't the stag party.

Don't be ashamed by your accent, either,
however thick it may be. The reception might
be at a country estate or Buckingham Palace but
that doesn't mean you need to radically change
the way you speak. If the bride and groom are
embarrassed by your thick Glasgow brogue,
they wouldn't have appointed you best man
in the first place.

Finding the right pace

If you're not 100 percent comfortable about speaking in public (i.e., you're a normal human being), then subconsciously you'll be keen to exit the limelight as soon as possible. Although you know you've got to make your words count, something at the back of your brain will be telling you to rattle through them quickly. The sooner you finish, the sooner you can hit the free bar, right?

Wrong. You've got to make this one count. You've got to deliver your speech at the appropriate speed.

Of course, everyone has their individual style of speaking. Quentin Tarantino rabbits on at about 1,000 words a minute. Princess Diana used to speak so slowly that you were always trying to finish the sentences for her. You've got to find somewhere in between. But, in general, it's much easier for your audience to follow if you slow things down.

Pause for breath in between sentences. At key stages in your speech, stop to look up at the guests. You can change the pace, too, for dramatic effect. You might be recounting an anecdote about the groom's sporting prowess, for example, or the time he got into a bar fight – both of which would benefit from a speedy delivery.

ENGAGING THE AUDIENCE

Never forget that you're a live act. It's essential you develop a relationship with your audience – hopefully a friendly one. OK, so you may not have the stage presence of Mick Jagger, but there are little tricks you can use to help you.

1. Remember that everyone wants you to fare well. You're a friend of the family. Just give them a bit of encouragement and they are sure to respond positively.

2. Before you start your speech, single out three people you know among the guests, preferably one on the left-hand side of the room, one in the middle and one on the right. During your speech, use these three people as security beacons. Every few minutes, look directly at one of them and smile. They will smile back and help your confidence. The other guests will think you are smiling at everyone in the room. You'll notice that politicians often do this during their rally speeches because it makes them appear more popular.

3. Sometimes you may feel your speech start to go a bit flat. There's a risk that a few of the guests might begin to lose interest. They may get fidgety or start chatting among themselves. The older ones might even doze off. Don't allow yourself to be put off, however. It's at this moment that you need to inject a bit of energy into your words. Try directing everyone's attention to the bride and groom again. Tell everyone what a beautiful and lucky couple they are, a comment that's sure to get a rousing cheer – just the type of positive energy that a flagging speech needs.

4. Some of your anecdotes are bound to involve other friends of the groom. If they're present among the guests, point them out. The more outgoing of the groom's buddies will love being mentioned in public, even if it's for slightly embarrassing reasons. Don't dig up too much dirt, though. Remember that when it comes to the stag party, what goes on tour, stays on tour. And whatever you do, don't ever mock the bridesmaids or members of the bride's family. That is certain to end in disaster.

5. Change your pace, pitch and volume (see
    page 121). Stand-up comics are masters of
    these techniques. Depending on the content of
    your speech and the type of anecdote you're
    telling, you may want to accelerate or slow
    down your delivery. You might alter the
    volume or pitch for dramatic effect, perhaps
    switching between a deep voice and a
    squeaky voice, or a shout and a whisper.
    Impersonations are always popular, too,
    even if they're wildly inaccurate. When
    telling stories about the groom, why not
    quote him directly and put on a funny voice
    to represent him?

6. How about some audience participation? This
    is the ultimate way to keep everyone engaged.
    Make them part of the act. You could conduct
    a brief awards ceremony, for example, handing
    out joke trophies to the guest who originally
    introduced the bride and groom, who travelled
    the furthest to attend the wedding, or to
    whomever is wearing the best hat or most
    flamboyant suit.

    An old favourite is the house key joke.
    Before the wedding, buy 10 blank keys from
    a key cutter. Just before the speeches start,
    surreptitiously hand out all the keys to some
    of the prettier girls among the guests and

Difficult audiences

It's a tough gig if you find yourself heckled. Why would a friend of the bride and groom want to interrupt you mid-speech? It's not like they've paid good money to see a show. It's more likely that someone will interrupt you with a private joke or what they think is a witty line. Even so, when you're mid-flow, it can be very off-putting indeed. You have two choices:

1. Completely ignore it, in which case you risk having the interruption repeated.
2. Acknowledge the speaker, thank them for their 'hilarious wit' and carry on talking.

Whatever you do, don't get into a protracted conversation with the heckler. If they persist, remind them that you have a very important speech to get through. Besides, the other guests will soon tell them to pipe down.

instruct them to keep quiet. Halfway through your speech, tell everyone that the bride knows the groom was quite a lothario in his youth but that she will forgive all his past escapades as long as ex-girlfriends present agree to hand back any keys they have to his house. It's at this point that the 10 pretty girls in question walk up to the stage and give back their keys. Cue much hilarity.

PHOTOS AND VIDEO

How many business presentations have you been to where the computers fail to work properly? And how utterly flustered has it made the presenter? For this reason, be very wary about using video technology during your speech. Wedding reception venues are not likely to have an IT specialist. Even if they do, you can hardly have everyone twiddle their thumbs while they wait for all the wires to be checked and the computer to be rebooted.

Keep it simple. Stills photography is much easier to handle. With help from the groom's family, you should be able to dig out some suitably embarrassing photos from his past. But think about how best to display them. Bear in mind that guests at the back of the room may struggle to see any photos that you choose to hold up.

Best man's checklist

Arm yourself with all these items on the morning of the wedding day and – hopefully – everything will go according to plan.

- [ ] Wedding schedule
- [ ] Phone numbers of all the ushers
- [ ] Names of immediate family of the bride and groom
- [ ] Wedding suit and accessories
- [ ] Buttonhole flowers
- [ ] Transport for you and the groom
- [ ] Cash (lots of it)
- [ ] Mints
- [ ] Umbrella
- [ ] Empty cans to tie to the back of the newlyweds' car
- [ ] Print-out of your speech
- [ ] The groom himself
- [ ] Oh, and last but most definitely not least: the ring

INDEX